Original title:
Poems from the Poplar Path

Copyright © 2025 Creative Arts Management OÜ
All rights reserved.

Author: Rosalie Bradford
ISBN HARDBACK: 978-1-80567-355-2
ISBN PAPERBACK: 978-1-80567-654-6

The Journey Where Roots Embrace

Under roots that wiggle and squirm,
Life's a dance, with laughter in form.
Silly squirrels spin tales of delight,
While ants march in time, oh what a sight!

The sunbeams giggle as they peek,
Tickling leaves, polite and meek.
Each step on this path brings a grin,
In this wacky world, let fun begin!

A Tapestry of Blossoms and Dreams

Petals wear hats made of dew,
While daisies prance in a hula-hoop too.
Colors clash in a zany parade,
Nature's canvas, oddly displayed!

Butterflies chat in whirlwind spins,
With jokes about caterpillars' silly sins.
Dreams bloom brightly, all out of line,
An uproar of blooms, all yours and mine!

Murmurs of the Ground Beneath

Listen close, the soil will share,
Tales of worms and their fuzzy hair.
A giggling rock, all covered in moss,
Claims to have won the great leaf toss!

Roots gossip and whisper with glee,
Trading secrets about you and me.
With chuckles and wiggles, they tease the breeze,
In this whimsical world, laughter's the keys!

The Twilight Trail of Forgotten Dreams

As shadows stretch and the moon does rise,
Old dreams waltz beneath starry skies.
The ghosts of hopes wear comical frowns,
Recalling their tales in giggly sounds.

On this trail, one might find,
Jokes lost in time, across the mind.
Each step echoes with whimsical cheer,
In twilight's glow, fun is always near!

Whispers Beneath the Canopy

A squirrel with a donut, oh what a sight,
It spins and it twirls, what a funny flight.
The birds all chuckle, 'What a snack!'
While the squirrel just grins, 'You can't have back!'

A rabbit hops by, with a twitchy nose,
It sneezes so loud, everyone knows.
The flowers all giggle, bending with glee,
As the rabbit looks puzzled, 'Was that me?'

Shadows of the Rustling Leaves

Beneath the trees, a picnic unfolds,
With ants stealing crumbs, oh the tales told.
The sandwich takes flight, chased by a bee,
While laughter erupts, 'Come back here, tea!'

A hedgehog arrives, in a top hat adorned,
Dancing with grace, although slightly scorned.
The leaves start to clap, what a curious scene,
As the hedgehog proclaims, 'I shall reign supreme!'

Echoes Along the Winding Trail

On the path ahead, a frog takes a leap,
Landing on a turtle, who wasn't asleep.
'Not my fault!' croaks the frog, 'I was aiming for flies!'
The turtle just grumbles, 'I'll take this in stride.'

A fox in a jacket, struts by with flair,
While the trees all gossip, 'Does he know who's there?'
But the fox winks cheekily, 'I'm on my own path!'
With the sun setting low, this is just my math!'

Secrets of the Ancient Grove

In the depths of the grove, a bear hums a tune,
Dancing with shadow, beneath the bright moon.
The trees tap their roots, keeping the beat,
While the deer join the dance, showing off their feet.

An owl starts to hoot, in rhythm so sly,
'You call that a dance? Come now, oh my!'
But the bear just laughs, with a grand twirl,
Saying, 'Join in the fun! Let's give it a whirl!'

Nature's Archive of Secrets

The squirrels gather, hats on tight,
Whispering tales of their nightly flight.
A chipmunk with glasses reads a map,
While birds in bow ties, dance and clap.

Leaves giggle softly, sharing the breeze,
As flowers toss jokes like skilled stand-up tease.
The brook chuckles, bubbling so bright,
Nature's a riot, what a delight!

Wading Through the Silver Rain

Raindrops wear shoes, tap dancing low,
 Puddles reflect a wild water show.
 Frogs with umbrellas leap in surprise,
While snails pull up, and dry their eyes.

The clouds play peek-a-boo, all around,
 A quirky parade in a merry-go-round.
 Dancing in splashes, what a fun sight,
 Wading through droplets, pure delight!

Evenings Draped in Salamander Dreams

Salamanders in pajamas, tell tales so grand,
Of moonlit adventures in a shimmering land.
Fireflies giggle like little bright chums,
While crickets keep rhythm, with tap-tap drums.

The stars spin stories, twinkling in glee,
As night wraps the forest in whimsy and spree.
Evenings so silly beneath a soft beam,
In the world of dreams, we all are supreme!

The Nest Where Stories Rest

A nest of laughter sits high in the tree,
Filled with odd tales from the buzz of the bee.
Chirps turn to chuckles, as owls take notes,
While critters in pajamas exchange funny quotes.

The wind spins yarns, whispers to the night,
Of mischief and magic, a laughing delight.
In this cozy nook, hilarity thrives,
Where stories have wings and happiness jives!

Brush of Petals on Skin

In the garden, bees take flight,
Tickling senses, what a sight!
Butterflies play tag with the breeze,
While I dodge ants with such unease.

Petals dance, on my nose they land,
A sneeze erupts, oh what a band!
Pollen swirls like confetti around,
Laughter echoes, nature's sound.

A squirrel giggles, it seems to know,
That nature's humor steals the show.
With every tumble, every slip,
The flower crowns my funny trip.

So here I sit, just me and jest,
In a world that loves to jest.
With petals brushing on my skin,
Life's comedy begins again!

Beneath the Dome of Earthly Embrace

Under the sky, I spy a clown,
Wearing weeds like a jester's crown.
His laughter rolls like thunder above,
As the earth below hums with love.

The trees stand tall, they shake their limbs,
Mimicking dance in nature's whims.
A rabbit prances, does the twist,
While I try hard not to be missed.

Grass tickles toes, the ants march in,
A parade of nature, ready to win.
Laughter rings out, it's quite absurd,
When a worm joins in, singing, "Herd!"

With every hug from soft, green blades,
Life's silliness never fades.
Beneath this dome where chuckles race,
Every moment's a funny chase!

A Lullaby of Leaf and Stone

As the leaves sway, a lullaby sings,
Nature's humor lightly clings.
Pebbles giggle, they bump and roll,
While grasshoppers jump, playing their role.

The wind whispers jokes to the trees,
Bending branches like playful knees.
A stone chuckles, lost in thought,
As a butterfly flutters, oh what a plot!

With each rustle, a laugh is shared,
Even the flowers seem unprepared.
They's dancing and twirling, quite a scene,
In the laughter of green, so serene.

So let the night bring stars that gleam,
With every chuckle, a gentle dream.
In lullabies of leaf and stone,
Nature's humor calls me home!

Tides of Time in Woodland Stillness

In the still woods, time takes a dip,
Where squirrels plot their acorn trip.
Mushrooms whisper secrets of old,
While the sun plays peek-a-boo, bold.

A brook chuckles, bubbling away,
While frogs jump in, ready to play.
They croak their jokes, one by one,
Nature's comedians under the sun.

The shadows stretch like rubber bands,
Tickling flowers with gentle hands.
Time does cartwheels, round and round,
In the peaceful woods, laughter's found.

So here we linger, lost in cheer,
With every giggle that draws us near.
In the tides of time, so light and free,
Nature's comedy is the best spree!

Beneath the Boughs of Memory

Under the trees, where laughter sings,
Squirrels debate on trivial things.
A nap is planned, but shoes take flight,
Do trees have ears? We think they might!

The bushes giggle, secrets they keep,
While ants march by, they just can't leap.
In this wild play, we joyfully roam,
With sticky fingers, this path feels like home.

Threads of Sunlight and Serenity

Sunbeams patchwork the fluttering ground,
As daisies wiggle, with joy they abound.
An unexpected tickle, a grasshopper's dance,
Caught in a giggle, we take our chance.

With butterflies prancing, and shadows that sway,
We trace silly shapes, in a whimsical play.
Who knew nature's stage could be such a blast?
With each little stumble, we find ourselves cast.

The Pathway of Silent Stories

Each step unfolds tales that trees whisper low,
Of mishaps and giggles from long, long ago.
A raccoon in shades, he winks as he steals,
Those snacks for the picnic, oh, what fun it feels!

The moon peeks through branches, with a wink and a grin,

As we play hide and seek, let the evening begin.
Fables of laughter, wrapped in the night,
With friends all around, everything feels right.

A Dance of Light Through the Foliage

A dance starts up as shadows take flight,
With leaves doing twirls in the shimmering light.
Laughter erupts as we join in the fun,
As fireflies flash like stars, one by one.

We spin and we twirl in the evening's embrace,
Tripping on roots, clouded with grace.
This merry-go-round of endless delight,
In the heart of the woods, everything feels right.

Guardians of the Gnarled Trunks

In the woods of whimsy, trees do dance,
Guardians giggle, given half a chance.
They tell jokes as shadows creep and crawl,
With bark-covered smiles, they charm us all.

Squirrels in bow ties, chitter and sway,
A council of branches leads the ballet.
Mossy old owls hoot out riddles loud,
While the roots below form a wiggly crowd.

A rabbit in slippers hops with delight,
They tip their hats to the moon's silver light.
Each gnarled trunk whispers tales of the past,
In this silly forest, the fun's unsurpassed.

With laughter and roots, they twine and twist,
Not a serious tree in this whimsical mist.
So wander on down to the giggling glade,
Where even the mushrooms are laughing, unafraid.

The Enchanted Passage of Time

In a land where clocks tick-tock absurd,
Time wears a bowler hat, flapping and blurred.
It stretches and bounces, just like a ball,
And laughter echoes down each twisting hall.

Yesterday's footsteps dance with delight,
While tomorrow giggles, peeking at night.
Today tries to juggle, but drops everything,
Chasing moments that fly away on the wing.

In this timeless place, please leave your shoes,
The floor will tickle you, you'll laugh or snooze.
Time does cartwheels and throws confetti,
Spinning into giggles, always ready, setty!

So join the parade of whimsical hours,
Where minutes bloom like bright, quirky flowers.
In the enchanted passage, forever we play,
As silly time prances, come join the ballet.

Nature's Canvas of Colors

In the meadow, colors wiggle and shout,
Crayons of nature scatter about.
The daisies wear hats, the sunflowers dance,
While butterflies giggle, caught in a trance.

Green grass giggles as breezes unfold,
With secrets of sunshine and stories retold.
The sky splashes blue on a canvas so wide,
With smirking clouds playing hide-and-seek, side to side.

A rainbow sprinkles joy after the rain,
Each drop a chuckle, each puddle a gain.
The trees toss confetti of leaves in the air,
Creating a party that's lively and rare.

So paint your heart with adventures anew,
In this crazy artwork of every hue.
Nature's funny canvas invites you to play,
Where laughter's the brushstroke that colors the day.

Starlit Promises Beneath the Sky

At night the stars chuckle, a twinkling spree,
Making silly faces from their heights so free.
They whisper sweet secrets to the wide, dark night,
As the moon does the limbo, a comical sight.

Dreams take a ride on back of a comet,
Painting the sky with each sparkling palette.
A shooting star zooms with a giggle and glide,
While stardust giggles sprinkle far and wide.

The owls hoot laughter, wise and a bit sly,
Not so serious under this playful sky.
They share goofy stories as they spin round,
While shadows on earth start to frolic around.

So lie on the grass and watch as they tease,
The cosmos is full of chuckles and ease.
Starlit promises twinkle, all merry and spry,
In the whimsical depths of the celestial pie.

Consolation of the Moonlit Veil

Under the moon's soft embrace,
A raccoon lost its way,
Stole my sandwich with a grin,
What a sneaky display!

Stars blink in playful delight,
As I chase him around,
Tripping over my own two feet,
What a sight I have found!

Laughter echoes through the night,
While he munches with glee,
Guess I'll have to share my snack,
With this furry decree!

But as dawn starts to break,
He bids me a quick adieu,
Leaving crumbs as memories,
Of the antics we both knew.

The Embrace of Nature's Breath

A squirrel in a ninja stance,
Leaps from tree to tree,
While I, a bumbling spectator,
Can't climb, but I can see!

Butterflies dance around me,
With such graceful flair,
I wave like an awkward mime,
They just swirl in the air!

The flowers gossip quietly,
About whom they might woo,
While bees steal all their secrets,
For some honey-thrift too!

Nature laughs at my attempts,
To blend in with the scene,
But in this funny playground,
It's the best I've ever been!

Memory Lane in Spring's Whisper

Dandelions sprout like popcorn,
Poking through the green grass,
I blow their seeds like wishes,
Hoping for a fun pass!

A dog barks at a butterfly,
And chases it with glee,
But trips over his own tail,
What a comical spree!

Kids ride bikes in a zigzag,
With squeals that fill the air,
One crashes in a puddle,
Splashed everywhere, a fair!

As spring whispers sweet secrets,
And giggles from afar,
Life's a joyful jigsaw,
With laughter as the star.

Mosaic of Colors Beneath the Sky

Painted skies at sunset glow,
Like a canvas gone awry,
As clouds create a funny face,
That makes us laugh, oh my!

A parade of colors follows,
In mismatched shoes they prance,
Roses red and violets blue,
Doing the happy dance!

The sun trips over hills so high,
As evening takes the stage,
While crickets tune their violins,
For nature's final page.

Stars wink like cheeky children,
Playing hide and seek,
In a mosaic of whimsy,
Where laughter is the peak.

Secrets of the Old Grove

In the old grove, secrets grow,
Squirrels chat in a playful show.
The owls hoot with laughing cheer,
As gossip spreads from ear to ear.

Trees whisper jokes in leafy tones,
While mushrooms giggle on their thrones.
A raccoon steals a curious glance,
And joins in for a woodland dance.

The breeze carries tales of fun,
When acorns roll from sun to sun.
Birds chirp each silly little rhyme,
As shadows play their tricks with time.

Underneath the old oak's shade,
Countless funny friends we've made.
In this grove where laughter thrives,
The secret lies in how we jive.

Echoes of the Windy Walk

On the windy walk, voices call,
The trees sway gently, having a ball.
With every gust, a joke takes flight,
As leaves tumble down in sheer delight.

A dandelion sneezes, oh, what a sight!
Spreading its seeds in a fluttering flight.
The path is lined with giggles galore,
As the wind whispers secrets, forevermore.

Each step brings a laugh, a sing-song rhyme,
Echoes of joy that tickle through time.
Socks and shoes dance without a care,
As puffs of air swirl about in the air.

Laughter rings out from high and low,
As friends on the path put on a show.
In every windblown twist and turn,
There's magic and mischief waiting to learn.

Leaves of Touch and Time

Leaves of green with stories to tell,
Whispering secrets under the spell.
They flutter and giggle, twirl in the breeze,
Creating a symphony that's sure to please.

With every pat, a rustle and rhyme,
Leaves share their tales like children in chime.
The story unfolds with each gentle touch,
A fun-loving dance that means so much.

The wise old willow smiles and sways,
As children chase shadows in sunlit plays.
The bark tells of pranks from long ago,
As laughter rings out with a joyful flow.

Under this canopy, friends come alive,
In a world where only joy can thrive.
Leaves of touch and time unite,
In the realm of giggles, everything's bright.

The Story of the Stray Stream

There once was a stream that loved to stray,
Wandering off in a silly way.
It giggled and splashed, quite in a whirl,
Leaving ripples of laughter in every swirl.

The fish had jokes and tossed them near,
As frogs croaked laughter, drawing cheer.
Each pebble had a tale to unfold,
Of fun, mischief, and moments bold.

As the sun sparkled on water's gleam,
The stray stream shared its silly dream.
Adventures flowed with a hop and a skip,
A giggly ride on a joyful trip.

So follow the stream where laughter beams,
In a world alive with fanciful dreams.
For in its watery wander, you will find,
The heart of fun that's one of a kind.

Woven Tales Among the Trunks

Beneath the trees, squirrels play,
Telling tales in a wacky way.
A raccoon winks, then starts to dance,
While birds critique him, at first glance.

The owls hoot with humor laced,
As chipmunks laugh, all interlaced.
The bark of trees holds secrets tight,
Of mischief felt in the soft night light.

Leaves rustle like the giggles near,
In a world where none live in fear.
Nature's jesters, bold and free,
Spin their yarns in harmony.

Roots that Hold the Earth

Roots dig deep, but what a sight,
Prefer to tickle, not to bite.
They laugh beneath the soil so dark,
Chatting with worms in a secret park.

Moles make puns about their height,
While ants debate who's got the might.
The grasses giggle in the breeze,
As dandelions tease and squeeze.

Fungi join the jovial crowd,
Poking fun, they're witty and loud.
With roots that grip the earth so tight,
The underground's a comical sight.

Journey Through the Dappled Light

In the forest of glowing beams,
The sun spills laughter in glittering streams.
A lizard does a somersault,
While shadows trip, in their own vault.

Butterflies flap, dressed to impress,
Swaying like they have no stress.
The pathway twists with giggles and glee,
Each step echoes joy, so carefree.

Crickets chirp their funny tunes,
As sunlight dances with silver spoons.
The journey's filled with charming sights,
Because laughter lives in the dappled lights.

The Dance of Soft Petals

Petals twirl in a breezy waltz,
One drops down and giggles, "Oops, my faults!"
A bee stumbles, too busy to chat,
Chasing the blooms like a comical cat.

The tulips gossip about the rose,
"Is that new perfume? Smells like a hose!"
A daisy laughs, while swinging its head,
A fashion show, where blooms are fed.

As petals dance under sunny skies,
The whole garden bursts with silly sighs.
In nature's theater, laughter is found,
A soft petal dance is joy unbound.

Frosted Dreams Along the Trail

Beneath the frost, the squirrels dance,
In search of nuts, they take a chance.
With tiny toes, they slip and slide,
Chasing each other, they giggle and glide.

A snowman's hat, too big, falls down,
As it rolls away, he wears a frown.
Mittens and scarves in a jolly mess,
Even the snowflakes start to confess.

The trees wear coats of white and gray,
They chuckle softly, come what may.
A rabbit hops over a snowdrift mound,
With a twitch of his nose, he spins around.

Frosted dreams in a winter's embrace,
Make every snowball a thrilling chase.
With laughter and cheer, the day drifts away,
As the sun pops out, they all yell, "Hooray!"

Spirits of the Whispering Woods

In the depths, where shadows play,
Ghostly giggles lead the way.
Branches sway in a cheeky dance,
Giving nature's critters a chance.

A raccoon's grin beneath the stars,
Sneaks off with snacks in little jars.
The owls hoot in a rhythmic cheer,
"Keep it down, or the bears will hear!"

Chirping crickets share their tunes,
With a wink, they play and swoon.
The moonlight glints on a playful hare,
Who pirouettes like he doesn't care.

The forest thrums with a lively sound,
Where whispers of joy are always found.
When day breaks, all spirits laugh aloud,
"Another adventure; let's make it loud!"

The Scent of Wildflowers and Woe

Among the blooms, a bee got stuck,
Wiggling free—"What rotten luck!"
Petals giggle with fragrant tease,
As he buzzes off, "Just let me sneeze!"

A butterfly flirts, it's true, it's bold,
With colors bright and stories told.
Yet tangled in stems, a fellow grump,
Complains of pollen and gives a huff.

Dandelions puff like little clouds,
As children blow, they gather crowds.
With giggles shared, they'll make a wish,
"Let's be silly, like a gummy fish!"

Though woes may linger, fun's the game,
In fields of laughter, who's to blame?
With scents that swirl beneath the sun,
Each day's a picnic, with more to come!

The Essence of an Autumn Stroll

Leaves crunch underfoot like pop rocks,
As squirrels plot beneath the clocks.
Strutting about with their little tails,
Snatching acorns, slipping on scales.

Pumpkin spice wafts through the air,
With giggles shared, folks do declare:
"Who needs a pie? Just give a wink,
And we'll have laughter before we think!"

Children race in hats too big,
Frolicking in the sun, they dig.
Rolling down hills without a care,
Leaving a trail of giggles in the air.

As twilight glows with comfy light,
Tales unfold, oh what a sight!
With marshmallows roasted, stories spun,
In this autumn stroll, we're all just fun!

A Tapestry of Briars and Blooms

In the garden, roses groan,
They found a thorny friend alone.
Bumbling bees are lost in thought,
Wondering why they can't be caught.

Weeds are dancing, quite absurd,
Their roots are tangled, that's the word.
While daisies gossip, soft and sweet,
Stumbling on each other's feet.

A daffodil in bright array,
Claims it can sing, but can't display.
With a wiggle and a flop,
It bows down low, then takes a hop.

Petunias plotting secret schemes,
In patterned bursts of vivid dreams.
Mixing colors, giggling loud,
Creating chaos, drawing a crowd.

Odes to the Inhabitant Skies

Clouds are saying silly jokes,
Like sneaky little playful folks.
One moody cumulus gripes and sighs,
While the sun just rolls its eyes.

Birds with hats are on a spree,
Perched on branches, filled with glee.
Fluttering tails and flappy wings,
Chirp about the silliest things.

A kite comes flying, having fun,
Saying, 'Look at me—I'm the one!'
Wiggling freely, catching air,
While giggling squirrels stare with flair.

Raindrops tap dance on the ground,
Splashing puddles all around.
In the sky, a rainbow beams,
Crafting laughter out of dreams.

A Journey Beyond the Bark

A squirrel donned a tiny cap,
Claiming he'd just had a nap.
Chasing friends through branches high,
With glitter scattered from the sky.

Beneath the trunk, a wise old frog,
Recites tales to a bouncing dog.
With every croak, the tales take flight,
Turning whispers into delight.

A chipmunk juggles acorns bold,
In a circus, brave and cold.
As nature cheers, it takes a bow,
Finding fame beneath the bough.

A spider spins its sticky thread,
Crafting a trap for crumbs of bread.
Giggles echo through the wood,
As critters muse on what is good.

Moonlight's Hand on Sleepy Bugs

When night descends, the crickets sing,
To sleepy bugs doing their thing.
A ladybug dreams of stars on high,
While fireflies waltz and flutter by.

A beetle playing hide and seek,
Under moonlight, finds its peak.
Each tense moment, a burst of cheer,
As the forest whispers, 'You are near.'

A tiny ant in pajamas snug,
Groans about the pesky jug.
While dormice snore, cocooned in leaf,
In a world of dreams, beyond belief.

With twinkling stars that gleam and glow,
The night wraps up in a cozy show.
Nature's laughter fills the air,
As moonlight casts its playful flair.

A Dance Where the Dew Meets Dawn

In the morning glow, they prance,
With dew on their shoes, it's quite a dance.
Squirrels in bowties, birds in hats,
Even rabbits try to avoid the spats.

The grass giggles beneath their feet,
As they twirl and hop to a comical beat.
A frog takes a leap, slips on a leaf,
Turns the cha-cha into a brief mischief.

Butterflies flutter, a clumsy crew,
While bees practice moves, all shiny and new.
With laughter booming, the dawn breaks free,
In a dance where the dew meets hilarity.

Pictures Painted in Twilight Hues

As the sun dips low, colors collide,
The owls hold a paintbrush, it's quite a ride.
Squirrels hang canvas, wide and bright,
While raccoons critique, in the fading light.

Pinks and purples splash like a dream,
While the stars chuckle at the artist team.
A fox struts over, tail held high,
Declaring he's ready for a twilight sky.

The moon yawns wide, giving a wink,
As brush strokes dance, and colors stink.
In this gallery made of giggles and sighs,
Each picture crafted earns laughter and cries.

The Lure of the Emerald Path

There's a winding path dressed in green,
Promises of snacks, a sight unseen.
Where turtles sip tea, and crickets sing,
You'll discover where silliness sprigs.

The trees gossip and giggle low,
Whispering secrets, just let it flow.
A deer with glasses reads the news,
It's a hoot, just check the morning hues.

At each bend, a funny surprise,
A hedgehog solves puzzles while everyone tries.
So follow the lures, don't miss the fun,
On the emerald path, laughter's never done.

Light Filtering Through the Leaves

As sunlight filters, creating spots,
The forest hosts its giggly thoughts.
Dancing shadows play hide and seek,
While critters hold court, just take a peek.

Breezes tell jokes, rustling the trees,
While branches sway with whimsical ease.
A chattering squirrel shares tales of lore,
That leave you laughing on the forest floor.

The dappled light, a canvas of cheer,
Spinning stories for everyone near.
With humor woven through every breeze,
These leaves will whisper just what you please.

The Language of Shifting Shadows

In the garden, shadows dance,
Swaying to an unseen chance,
A squirrel debates his next big leap,
While the cat plots slumber, not a peep.

The trees conspire in whispers low,
A breeze comes by with a jaunty flow,
A leaf falls down, just like a hat,
"What's next?" it asks, the world is flat.

The sun plays tag with clouds so bright,
Dodging raindrops on a silly flight,
While birds compose a cheeky tune,
Swapping jokes with the lazy moon.

Even the flowers join the jest,
Wobbling heads on nature's quest,
They giggle as the wind runs wild,
This entire place is nature's child.

A Canvas of Nature's Narrative

In the meadow, colors collide,
A bluebird in plaid, what a wild ride,
Sunflowers strut, their faces so bold,
Telling secrets only they unfold.

The brook chuckles, splashes with glee,
Mossy stones grin, quite carefree,
A painter with splatters of mud and cheer,
Crafting a scene that's whimsically clear.

Butterflies twirl in glorious brawl,
Chasing each other with giggles and squall,
Pollen dusted wings like confetti in air,
Nature's own party, a grand affair.

Bumbles buzz in a doorway dance,
Chasing each other, taking a chance,
While daisies plot how to snatch some sun,
Creating chaos just for fun.

Between Earth and Ethereal

Fairies giggle in the twilight glow,
Painting skies with a flamboyant show,
While critters below find mischief to seek,
A hedgehog in sneakers, quite unique.

Stars peek down with a twinkle and wink,
"What's in the plan?" they softly think,
While owls wear glasses, reading the night,
Sipping moonlight like it's a delight.

Clouds drift by with a playful sigh,
Changing shapes to wave hello or goodbye,
A dragon forms, then turns into cheese,
Nature's own riddle that aims to please.

The breeze brings laughter wrapped in light,
Tickling the trees till they giggle outright,
Frolicsome echoes of whispers sweet,
A world alive, where fun and magic meet.

Sighs of the Twilight Breeze

As day bids night a saucy adieu,
The breeze carries whispers, old yet new,
Crickets strum on their tiny strings,
While fireflies dress up, adorning like kings.

A raccoon sings a tuneful song,
Poking at shadows that dance along,
With every step comes a chuckle or two,
"Hey, who's that? Oh! It's just you!"

The moon winks down with a silver grin,
Encouraging laughter where mischief begins,
A flower sways with a haughty flair,
"Not tomorrow, I'd rather not share!"

The night unfolds its funny tales,
Of frolicsome felines and little snails,
In this twilight where giggles float free,
Nature's party, just wait and see.

Conversations with the Whispering Woods

In the woods, the trees all chatter,
Discussing which squirrel is fatter.
Leaves giggle as they shake in glee,
Whispering secrets of the bee.

A chipmunk joins with a tiny cheer,
Claiming he's the best comedian here.
The owls hoot with sage advice,
While crickets plan a dance that's nice.

Sunlight dapples with a wink,
Making shadows that twist and shrink.
The brook chuckles as it flows,
Adding rhymes that nobody knows.

With every breeze, a funny tale,
Of how a fox slipped on a snail.
In this grove of chortles and quips,
Nature has the best comic scripts.

The Lullaby of the Wandering Breeze

The breeze floats by with a mischievous grin,
   Tickling the flowers, and then it spins.
  It whispers to daisies, "Don't be so shy!"
  "Wave your petals or I'll pass you by!"

  A butterfly giggles, "I'm on a quest!
  To find the flower that's truly the best!"
The breeze just chuckles, "Oh, what a game,
  Your beauty, dear friend, is not for fame!"

The clouds drift lazily, yawning with glee,
"Who knew the earth could be so funny?"
The sun peeks out, throws a spotlight wide,
  As the breeze invites all to join the ride.

  Together they dance, a whimsical show,
   With laughter that sparkles from below.
A serenade woven through branches and reeds,
   In this silly ballet, nature proceeds.

Hues of Change Along the Way

Autumn paints the trees with zest,
Orange and red, they wear their best.
The leaves giggle as they drift down slow,
"A fashion statement? You bet! We glow!"

Winter grumbles, "I'm here to freeze,
But look! The snowflakes dance with ease!"
They tumble and play on the icy floor,
While mice in hats try to dance and soar.

Spring pops in, with colors so bright,
"Hold your applause, I've taken flight!"
The flowers bicker; "Who's the star?"
"I am, no wait, I'm the best by far!"

Summer sizzles, "Let's have some fun,
I bring the heat and a beach for everyone!"
The sunbeams wink, their warmth is a blast,
In this riot of colors, good times are vast!

Breath of the Earth: A Reverie

The earth lets out a comical sigh,
As ants march past with a grand ol' cry.
"Load up the crumbs, we're having a feast!"
"Make way, make way! Here comes the least!"

A worm pokes out, "Can't find my hat!"
As the ground chuckles, "You look good like that!"
Even the rocks join the merry spree,
"Moss on our backs? Oh, don't you agree?"

The flowers gossip, they're full of delight,
"Who wore it better, the rose or the kite?"
With every rustle, the forest chimes,
In this silly world, laughter climbs.

So here's to the earth, with a wink and a cheer,
In its embrace, let's gather near.
Fun fills the air, and joy cascades,
In the symphony of life, the laughter invades.

Reflections in the Pool of Calm

In the pond where ducks swim round,
I ponder on thoughts that make no sound.
A frog croaks loud, a fish just flips,
I laugh so hard, I nearly trip.

The clouds above are in a race,
Chasing their dreams, a fluffy chase.
A squirrel stops, looks up at me,
I wink back, both feeling free.

Ripples dance like a happy tune,
A turtle bobs, snoring at noon.
Should I throw a pebble or two?
Nah, he'll wake up, and that won't do!

In this calm pool, life's absurd,
Each little splash is quite unheard.
Here I sit with my thoughts that swirl,
Just me and nature, what a world!

Fragments of Forgotten Footsteps

Scattered trails where friends once played,
With silly games and pranks they made.
A shoe sits lonely, oh what a sight,
Did it run away or just take flight?

Leaves whisper tales of giggles past,
In the corners where shadows cast.
A snack half-eaten by a tree,
Mr. Squirrel, that's too bold of thee!

Footprints fade like a winking star,
Chasing dreams, not going far.
Oh, to be light and free like air,
To dance on paths without a care!

In this park where laughter stitched,
Every moment we joyfully twitched.
Fragments left for birds to find,
A puzzle piece of the silly kind.

Traces of Time in Bark and Leaf

Tree trunks wear their age with pride,
With grooves and notches, their stories hide.
A passed-on note says 'I was here',
But who wrote that? It's rather queer!

Leaves flutter down like paper planes,
Bouncing off my head, oh what pains!
The wind, it giggles, gives a shove,
A tumbleweed flies — guess it's in love?

Nature's scribbles on bark and branch,
A dance of shadows, a sunny ranch.
Each knot and twist, a mystery spins,
What is the secret the forest wins?

As time rolls on, they stand as guides,
In laughter's whisper, the past resides.
Let's climb a tree, let's take a look,
Adventure awaits, come read this book!

The Invitation of the Winding Way

Curves and bends invite a stroll,
With every twist, my thoughts unroll.
The path ahead, a playful tease,
Turns and loops like a silly breeze.

A rabbit hops with a cheeky flair,
As if to say, 'Come join me, bear!'
I chase after, but he's too quick,
Laughing at my slowest trick.

Bumps and dips, oh what a ride,
Every step, I miss the guide.
Who needs a map when trees can talk?
Each route a friend, let's have a walk!

So here I wander, what a maze,
With silly thoughts and sunny days.
The winding way calls, sing along,
In this laugh-filled path, we all belong!

A Soliloquy of Starlit Silence

In the quiet night, a frog sings loud,
Murmuring tales to a curious crowd.
Stars twinkle back with a mischievous grin,
Wondering just where all this noise has been.

A cat on a fence, watching with glee,
Wonders if frogs might make good tea.
The moon comes out, rolls its eyes in jest,
Thinking of all who can't seem to rest.

Crickets join in, adding to the hum,
While owls hoot softly, "What's become of fun?"
Laughter echoes through the shadowed trees,
As fireflies dance with whimsical ease.

So here we are under this vast sky,
Sharing goofy secrets, you and I.
In starlit silence, we find our jest,
Doing nothing, yet feeling our best.

Portraits of the Wandering Breeze

A breeze flutters by, with a wink and a swirl,
Tugging at hats, making skirts twirl.
It's playing tag with the leaves on the run,
Causing mischief while having some fun.

The flowers all giggle, their petals do sway,
As the breeze whispers softly, "Let's dance today!"
But bees take their time, in pollen they bask,
Wondering who thought of this wild, foolish task.

Clouds laugh above as they drift through the blue,
Chasing each other—what a comical view!
A squirrel drops acorns, then starts to prance,
Thinking the breeze just invited to dance.

So let's twirl with the wind, give a shout,
As the wandering breeze takes us all about.
Life's too short for a frown or a pout,
Join the playful air and let laughter sprout!

Murmurs of the Shared Path

On a winding path where the hedgehogs roll,
Two squirrels debate who shall make the first stroll.
One takes a leap, the other stands still,
Contest of the bravest, sheer will versus thrill.

With each tiny footprint, stories unfold,
Of cats in the night and of critters so bold.
A misstep here, oh! Rocks underfoot,
Risking a tumble, they blame it on the root!

Jokes fly like acorns tossed in the air,
As the path leads on, without a care.
A turtle joins in, slow and aloof,
Declaring it's better to have fun than goof!

So here on this trail, laughter fills the space,
While nature joins in this hilarious race.
In the murmuring woods, we share our tales,
With giggles and grins as our laughter prevails.

Beneath the Verdant Veil

Beneath leafy branches, the stories take flight,
Where a rabbit dreams big in the soft moonlight.
He's plotting a journey, quite grand in design,
To find the best patch of carrots to dine.

A crow caws loudly, "What's taking so long?"
While the rabbit starts humming a cheeky little song.
"Don't rush my plans, I'm the king of this space,
With a tummy that rumbles, I must keep good pace!"

The grass nods in rhythm, a wave in the breeze,
While ants march in line, each carrying cheese.
The rabbit just chuckles, "Look at them go,
With teamwork and snacks, they're putting on quite the show!"

So underneath leaves, with laughter we dwell,
Sharing sweet moments, oh, wouldn't it swell?
In the heart of the woods, let each day unveil,
A treasure of giggles beneath verdant veil.

Light's Play Through the Foliage

The sun peeks through leaves with a grin,
Casting shadows where mischief begins.
Squirrels chase each other in silly delight,
While birds plot their schemes with a flap and a flight.

Breezes tickle branches, a rustling sound,
Nature's giggles are all around.
Dancing dandelions sway without care,
As butterflies laugh in the warm summer air.

A tree with a knot seems to chuckle with glee,
While ants hold a parade, oh, what a spree!
Laughter grows louder, a chorus, a song,
In this playful realm, we all do belong.

So come join the fun beneath the green crown,
Where joy is a treasure and never a frown.
With light's playful dance, let our spirits soar,
In this whimsical wood, there's always more!

Harmony Found in Nature's Laughter

In the meadow of mirth, where daisies joke,
Each petal a giggle, a humorous poke.
The brook's bubbling laughter, a ticklish tune,
Sings to the stars, beneath the bright moon.

Grasshoppers play hopscotch on sunlit ground,
While frogs in tuxedos croak, buoyant sound.
A squirrel spins stories with magnificent flair,
While the wise old owl just laughs at the air.

The wind starts to tease, it tickles the trees,
Nature's chorus of chuckles floats with ease.
As petals pirouette in a whimsical dance,
Life's little wonders give us a chance.

So let's join the song of this jovial space,
With humor and laughter, we quicken our pace.
In harmony, we find the joy of the day,
Where nature's sweet laughter leads us away.

Tales Written in Branches

The branches are scribes, inscribing the tales,
Of cheeky chipmunks and gusty gales.
Each twig a story, each leaf a jest,
Nature's memoirs in a colorful fest.

The wise old tree whispers secrets of cheer,
Of funny little critters that wander near.
A raccoon in pajamas, quite snug in his den,
Swaps stories with the fox of a jam with a hen.

Beneath the tall elms, laughter never lacks,
As the kittens play tag with their doggy friends' backs.
Each rustle a giggle, each rusting leaf,
Echoes of joy, in the green, we believe.

So gather around for this whimsical show,
Where branches hold tales of the laughter we know.
With nature's fair shimmer, let's listen and laugh,
For every tall tree holds an amusing paragraph.

The Resonance of Quiet Moments

In the hush of the glen, a whisper is heard,
As crickets recount tales without any word.
A slow breeze tiptoes, its laughter contained,
While the moon shares a wink, its silence ingrained.

Pebbles giggle softly, a chuckle below,
As ripples dance lightly in the water's flow.
A quiet serenade from daisies in bloom,
Is nature's sweet joke that lifts all gloom.

Beneath the calm skies, where the shadows play,
The humor of stillness finds its own way.
And in the stillness, oh what we can glean,
Are echoes of laughter in spaces serene.

So cherish each moment, for laughter will rise,
In the quietest places beneath the vast skies.
For in silence, we find a whimsical art,
That tickles the soul and warms every heart.

Horizons Seen Through Nature's Lens

A squirrel in shades, quite a sight,
He poses, strikes a quirky flight.
The trees applaud with rustling cheer,
As grasshoppers chime in, oh dear!

A crow caws loud, with flair so grand,
It thinks it rules this leafy land.
But in the breeze, a butterfly flies,
With laughter twinkling in its eyes.

A pond reflects a moonlit joke,
Where frogs play cards and giggle as they croak.
The reeds shimmy to the rhythm divine,
Nature's laughter; it's all by design.

So here we roam, both wild and free,
Making memories as light as can be.
In a world where the silly meets the wise,
Through nature's lens, oh how we rise!

A Reverie Among Wisps of Cloud.

Clouds in hats drift by so slow,
A sheepdog grins, it steals the show.
A sunny patch for those on high,
Where daisies wiggle, oh my, oh my!

Balloons float gently, lost in dreams,
While giggling leaves float on sunbeams.
A bumblebee tries to steal a kiss,
But ends up tangled, what a bliss!

A picnic spread, but ants arrive,
In tiny suits, they strive and thrive.
They dance around, declare a feast,
While we just laugh, our joy released.

So let's not fret over clouds above,
These wisps bring laughter, peace, and love.
Each puff a story, each shadow a game,
In reverie we revel, wild and untame!

Whispers Beneath the Canopy

Under green caps where secrets gleam,
The whispers gather, a quirky team.
A ladybug shares a juicy tale,
While owls hoot softly, never stale.

Mushrooms chit-chat, they're all aglow,
A wise old fern gives a friendly elbow.
The roots all gossip beneath the ground,
With chuckles and snickers, a joyful sound.

Light beams play, a shadowed ballet,
Where squirrels compete in a nut-filled fray.
The canopy giggles, a rustling muse,
While dangling moss enjoys the views.

In this realm of whimsy, we join the fun,
With branches waving, a wild run.
Whispers intertwine, a merry dance,
In nature's hold, we take our chance!

Shadows Dance on the Trail

Footsteps echo, the shadows prance,
A line of ants in a goofy dance.
With sticks as drums and leaves for cheer,
Nature's band works, never fear!

The sunlight flickers, a jumping game,
Where rabbits hop and never feel shame.
A toad on the log sings out a tune,
As butterflies swoon under the moon.

Round every bend, a chuckle awaits,
With trees that tease and jittery mates.
A fox twirls about, all wrapped in glee,
In this wonderland, we feel so free.

So here we wander, laughter in tow,
With shadows dancing, stealing the show.
Each step a jest, on paths so wide,
With nature's joy, we take the ride!

The Heartbeat of the Forest Floor

Beneath the trees, the creatures hide,
They dance and prance, with nothing to bide.
A squirrel jokes, with acorn in tow,
Says, "It's my snack—don't you even know?"

The bunnies hop with laughter so bright,
While bugs perform in a comical flight.
A turtle shouts, "I'm fast as a storm!"
The others chuckle, "You should conform!"

Worms wiggle underfoot in delight,
Claiming they're gymnasts, oh what a sight.
The forest floor, a laugh-filled retreat,
Where every heartbeat is silly and sweet.

Reflections in the Stream of Time

In the stream, the fish don glasses and stare,
"Who's that swimmer? They've got quite the flair!"
A frog just snorts, "That's not how you do!"
While the ripples laugh at the passerby crew.

A turtle floats by, wearing a top hat,
Says, "Greetings, dear friends! Now, how about that?"
The water reflects quite the whimsical beat,
Making us all feel silly and neat.

As time flows by, with a splish and a splash,
The giggles abound, with every wild flash.
The moments drift lightly, just silly little rhymes,
With each quirky reflection, we cherish our times.

Swaying to the Song of the Wind

The trees do a jig, oh what a sight,
Leaves laughing hard in the clear daylight.
The whispering wind has a joke to share,
Sways all the branches, swings through the air.

A gust blows past, tickles the ground,
The flowers giggle, their colors abound.
"Can you believe it?" they all start to sway,
"Wind's got the moves; let's dance all day!"

The branches creak with a comedic twist,
While the sun tries hard to keep up with this.
Swaying and laughing, a forest parade,
In every soft breeze, a fun serenade.

Flickers of Hope in Dappled Shade

Under the leaves, a shadowy game,
The rabbits hop, no two are the same.
A deer trips lightly, says, "Whoops! My bad!"
The shadows all giggle, isn't that rad?

The sunlight dances, playing hide and seek,
While chattering chipmunks playfully squeak.
"Have you seen Charlie?" one whispers with grace,
"He's lost in the shadows, the poor little face!"

Yet flickers of hope in the glades abound,
With laughter and joy, in every soft sound.
In the dappled shade, all worries decay,
As friends gather round for some fun in the day.

The Lament of Exposed Roots

Oh dear roots, why spread so wide?
Caught in the open, you've nowhere to hide.
Gossipy winds laugh at your plight,
Yet still you cling, holding on tight.

A squirrel once tried to stake a claim,
But tripped on your strands, and oh what a shame!
Now you're the punchline for every jest,
Yet you stay grounded, perhaps for the best.

Whispers of the Living Canopy

Up in the branches, the gossiping leaves,
Share tales of the birds and the other reprieves.
"Did you hear what the owl said last night?"
"A hoot too many, but still quite a sight!"

The branches shake with laughter so free,
As acorns fall down, landing with glee.
The sunlight winks through the small gaps above,
While squirrels debate what they truly love.

Fragments of Time Amidst the Lichen

Lichen, oh ancient, with stories to tell,
You cling to rocks like a stubborn spell.
Your greenish hue masks a quirky delight,
As you party with spores in the soft, moonlit night.

Each crack in the stone is a time-travel pass,
To when woolly mammoths strolled on the grass.
But here you are, with a joke on repeat,
Telling moss to lighten up, isn't life sweet?

The Allure of the Wandering Wood

In the forest where paths twist and tangle,
A woodpecker's beat is quite the jangle.
Leaves dance around like they own the place,
Reminding the lost ones to pick up the pace.

With each step, a twig snaps like a joke,
"Did you hear about the toad? What a bloke!"
And the trees chuckle, sharing in mirth,
As creatures unite in this magical birth.

Gardens That Have Lost Their Stories

Once bloomed tales in blossoms bright,
Now weeds wear crowns in shady light.
The gnomes have gone, they're on a spree,
Gardens lost in mockery.

The roses sigh with every breeze,
While carrots play hide and seek with peas.
"I swear I saw a sunflower grin!"
Nature's circus, let the games begin!

The squirrels roll dice beneath the trees,
While pigeons plot to steal the keys.
With soil rich in fanciful schemes,
These gardens host our silliest dreams.

So come, dear friend, with laughter's spark,
Join the dance till it gets dark.
For in this place where chaos reigns,
We'll find the joy that still remains.

The Colours of Lingering Silence

A blue that giggles, a red that sings,
Even gray can wear a pair of wings.
The walls twist into a funny shape,
Whispers pink as they escape.

In corners hide shades of chuckling dreams,
Where each hue bursts at the seams.
The quiet shouts through vibrant brush,
A rainbow's laughter in a soft hush.

Forget the hush of bland old white,
Violet pranks leap into sight.
Yellow tickles the golden sun,
In this palette, we're all having fun.

So paint your world in spontaneous glee,
Let every color dance wild and free.
For silence here has a funny twist,
In hues of joy, we can't resist.

Notes Carried by the Gentle Zephyr

A breeze that tickles, a laugh that flies,
Whispers secrets and puzzled sighs.
It carries notes of a missing hat,
And giggles through the fields like a cat.

It juggles leaves from tree to tree,
And makes the flowers flip with glee.
The songs it sings are silly and sweet,
As butterflies dance on fleeting feet.

"Hey there, wind, won't you stay awhile?"
It twirls and spins with a cheeky smile.
Catching jokes from fields afar,
A rollicking breeze, the brightest star!

So listen close with an open heart,
For in the whispers, we all play a part.
With every note the zephyr sends,
A world of laughter never ends.

The Echoes of Yesterday's Reverie

In the attic lies a wondrous tale,
Of socks that danced on a windy gale.
The echoes giggle, the memories sway,
As yesterday's dreams come out to play.

A rubber chicken struts with flair,
Chasing shadows without a care.
Laughter bounces off each aged wall,
In this whimsical space, we rise and fall.

Old photographs whisper jokes from years,
And teddy bears chuckle amidst our tears.
With every echo, a smile it brings,
In forgotten corners, the past still sings.

So let us dance with echoes bold,
In dreams of gold, let the stories unfold.
For in laughter, time ceases to bind,
As echoes of joy are lovingly entwined.

www.ingramcontent.com/pod-product-compliance
Lightning Source LLC
Chambersburg PA
CBHW071829160426
43209CB00003B/247